Symbols of Canada

Animals

Edited by Deborah Lambert

Weigl

Published by Weigl Educational Publishers Limited
6325 10 Street SE
Calgary, Alberta
T2H 2Z9

www.weigl.com

Library and Archives Canada Cataloguing in Publication data available upon request.
Fax 403-233-7769 for the attention of the Publishing Records department.

ISBN 978-1-55388-924-3 (hard cover)
ISBN 978-1-55388-930-4 (soft cover)

Printed in the United States of America
1 2 3 4 5 6 7 8 9 0 13 12 11 10 09

Editor: Heather C. Hudak
Design: Kathryn Livingstone

All of the Internet URLs given in the book were valid at the time of publication. However, due to the dynamic nature
of the Internet, some addresses may have changed, or sites may have ceased to exist since publication. While the author
and publisher regret any inconvenience this may cause readers, no responsibility for any such changes can be accepted
by either the author or the publisher.

Every reasonable effort has been made to trace ownership and to obtain permission to reprint copyright material. The publishers
would be pleased to have any errors or omissions brought to their attention so that they may be corrected in subsequent printings.

Weigl acknowledges Getty Images as its primary image supplier for this title.
Alamy: pages 17, 23 bottom left.

We gratefully acknowledge the financial support of the Government of Canada through the Book Publishing Industry Development
Program (BPIDP) for our publishing activities.

Contents

Ontario

Northwest Territories

Saskatchewan

Prince Edward Island

Nunavut

Quebec

Yukon

What are Symbols?

A symbol is an item that stands for something else. Objects, artworks, or living things can all be symbols. Every Canadian province and territory has official symbols. These items represent the people, history, and culture of the provinces and territories. Symbols of the provinces and territories create feelings of pride and citizenship among the people who live there. Each of the ten provinces and three territories has chosen animal, or **faunal**, symbols to represent it.

Creating a Faunal Symbol

In most cases, faunal symbols refer to animals. In Canada, faunal symbols are chosen from among the animals of the country, province, and territory that they are meant to represent. Traditionally, the animals chosen as faunal symbols are commonly found throughout the region it represents. However, animals that are not **indigenous** to the region may be chosen for historical reasons. Faunal symbols can be recognized for historic, religious, or other reasons.

Canada's national animal, the beaver, is featured on the five-cent coin.

Locating Provinces and Territories

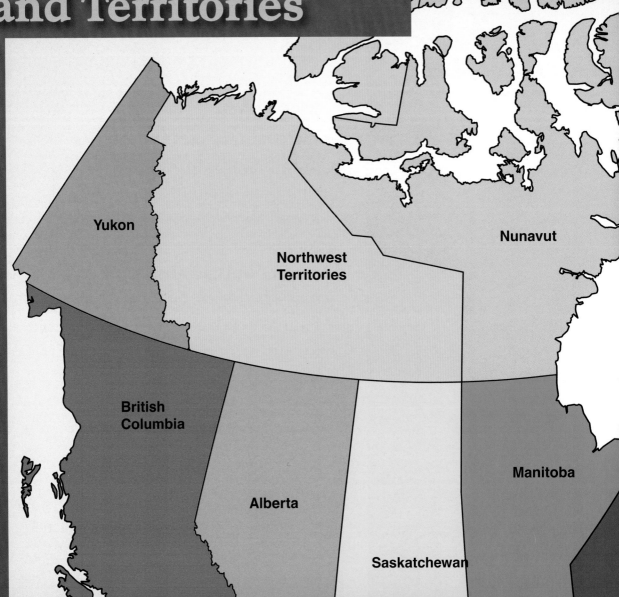

Each province and territory has a faunal symbol. Each province and territory is unique because of its land, people, and wildlife. Throughout this book, the provinces and regions are colour coded. To find an animal symbol, first find the province or territory using the map on this page. Then, turn to the pages that have the same colour province or territory image in the top corner.

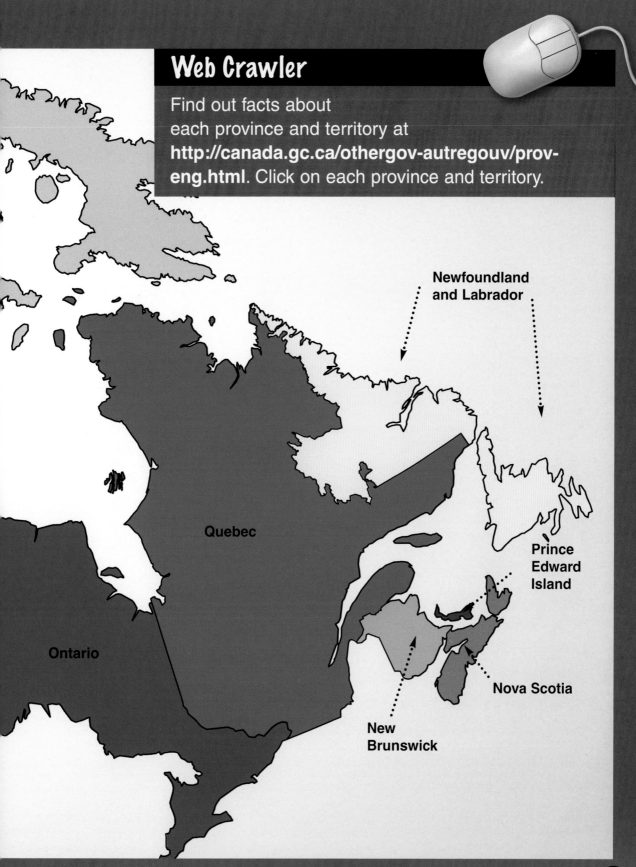

Web Crawler

Find out facts about each province and territory at **http://canada.gc.ca/othergov-autregouv/prov-eng.html**. Click on each province and territory.

Newfoundland and Labrador

Quebec

Prince Edward Island

Ontario

Nova Scotia

New Brunswick

Canada's Land and People

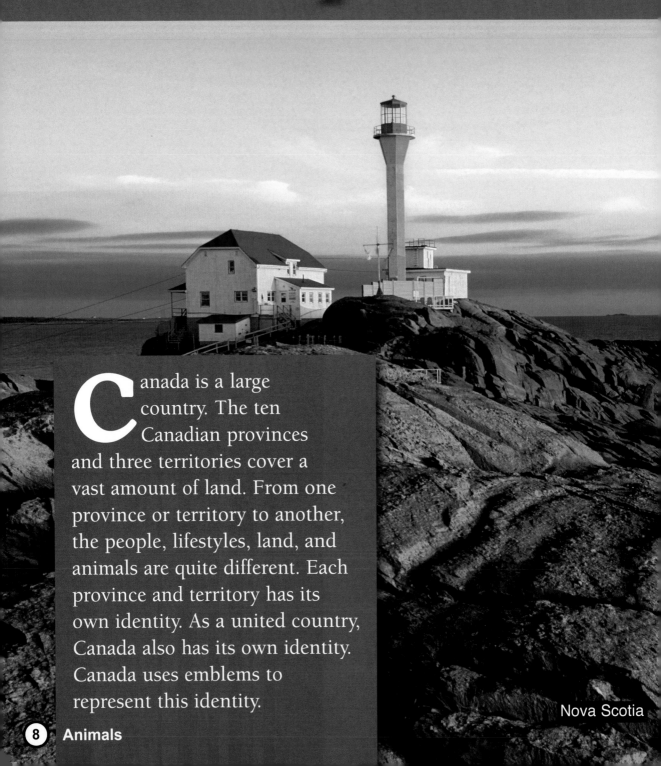

Canada is a large country. The ten Canadian provinces and three territories cover a vast amount of land. From one province or territory to another, the people, lifestyles, land, and animals are quite different. Each province and territory has its own identity. As a united country, Canada also has its own identity. Canada uses emblems to represent this identity.

Nova Scotia

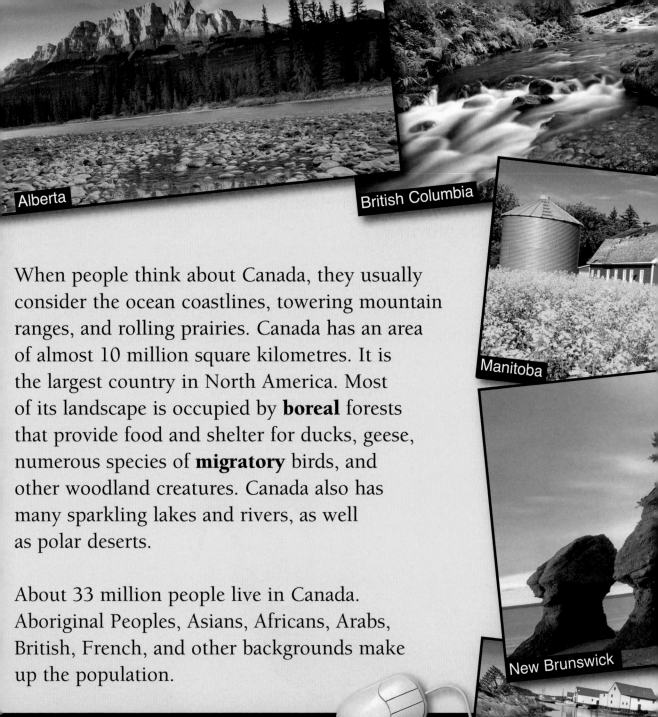

Alberta

British Columbia

Manitoba

New Brunswick

Newfoundland and Labrador

When people think about Canada, they usually consider the ocean coastlines, towering mountain ranges, and rolling prairies. Canada has an area of almost 10 million square kilometres. It is the largest country in North America. Most of its landscape is occupied by **boreal** forests that provide food and shelter for ducks, geese, numerous species of **migratory** birds, and other woodland creatures. Canada also has many sparkling lakes and rivers, as well as polar deserts.

About 33 million people live in Canada. Aboriginal Peoples, Asians, Africans, Arabs, British, French, and other backgrounds make up the population.

Web Crawler

Trace important events in the history of Canada at **www.cyber-north.com/canada/history.html**.

Discover Canada's natural wonders by clicking the numbers on the map of Canada at **www.thecanadian encyclopedia.com/customcode/Media.cfm?Params= A3natural-wonders.swf**.

Alberta

The Rocky Mountain bighorn sheep became Alberta's official animal symbol on August 18, 1989. These animals have lived in Alberta for thousands of years. Their prehistoric bones have been found throughout the province.

Alberta was once home to the largest bighorn sheep herds in the world. Today, there are about 5,800 of these animals in Alberta. Bighorn sheep live mostly in the province's Rocky Mountains. However, they can be found throughout the mountains of western North America and as far south as Mexico.

British Columbia

The spirit bear, also known as the Kermode bear, was named the official animal symbol of British Columbia in April 2006. It is found mostly on the province's central and northern coasts.

Though the spirit bear is white in colour, it is not **albino**. It is a black bear that has white fur due to a rare **genetic** trait. According to **First Nations** beliefs, the area where the spirit bear lives was once covered in ice. Raven, the Creator, made the land lush and green for the people. To remind the people of the ice cold, Raven left every tenth bear white.

Spirit Bears are omnivores. This means they eat both meat and plant matter. Plants, such as berries, nuts, fruits, roots, and grasses, as well as insects, deer, moose fawns, **carrion**, and salmon make up most of their diet.

Manitoba

The bison is Manitoba's animal symbol. It is an important symbol of Manitoba's heritage. Also known as buffalo, the bison is a large animal with a shaggy, dark-brown mane. Its humped shoulders and short legs are covered with hair. The bison's coat is very thick. This helps to keep it warm in cooler temperatures. In the summer months, it sheds this coat to keep cool.

Two hundred years ago, tens of thousands of bison lived on the Manitoba prairies. Today, most bison live in national parks because large parts of Manitoba's prairies have been turned into farmland. Manitoba is home to the third-largest bison herd in Canada, after Alberta and the Northwest Territories.

Bison were important to Aboriginal Peoples for survival. They ate meat from the bison and its dried skins were used to make blankets, clothing, and teepees. Aboriginal Peoples used the bison's bones to make weapons and tools.

New Brunswick

Though New Brunswick does not have an official animal symbol, many animals call this province home. Some animals fly through the air, some swim through the water, and many more live deep in the province's forests. The larger animals in the forests include black bears, moose, white-tailed deer, and wildcats, such as lynx. There are also smaller animals, such as flying squirrels, martens, minks, muskrats, rabbits, and skunks.

The province also has a large assortment of marine life. At least 12 different species of whale pass by New Brunswick every year looking for food. American lobsters live in New Brunswick's coastal waters. They are found at the bottom of the sea, usually at depths of 3 to 720 metres.

Newfoundland and Labrador

The Newfoundland dog is one of Newfoundland and Labrador's two animal symbols. These dogs have thick, black coats that keep them warm during the province's cold winters and rainy season. They are very good swimmers, and in the past, fishers used them to help pull in nets filled with fish.

Newfoundland ponies are important to the province's history. The 1996 Heritage Animals Act protects these winter-hardy animals because their **breed** is disappearing. Today, fewer than 200 Newfoundland ponies exist.

Northwest Territories

Like New Brunswick, the Northwest Territories does not have an official animal symbol. The polar bear is important to the Northwest Territories. It is shown on a flag that flies over government buildings, and the territory's license plates are in the shape of a polar bear.

Polar bears are specially adapted for life in the Northwest Territories. Their feet are webbed, like flippers, to help them swim in the Arctic Ocean, where they hunt seals. Their fur is **waterproof**. It is made of clear, hollow tubes that draw in the Sun's heat. The bottom of their paws is covered in fur to keep them from slipping on the ice.

The province also is home to Arctic foxes, caribou, grizzly bears, and muskoxen. Seals and walruses, as well as narwhals and other whales, swim in the Arctic Ocean.

Nova Scotia

Nova Scotia's official animal is the duck tolling retriever, or duck toller. It was named the province's official dog in 1995.

This medium-sized dog was first bred in Nova Scotia in the early 1800s. It is the smallest breed of retrievers. Most duck tollers are red or orange in colour, with white markings on their chest, paws, and tail. Duck tollers are smart, fast dogs. They help hunters catch ducks by running and playing along Nova Scotia's shoreline. This causes the ducks to move closer to the shore and to hunters.

Nunavut

Nunavut's animal symbol, the Canadian Inuit dog, also known as the qimmiq, was chosen as the territory's official animal on May 1, 2000.

The Canadian Inuit dog was chosen to be the official animal because it is important to Inuit survival. It has provided transportation in the Arctic for thousands of years. This medium-sized, **robust** dog pulls sleds, helps hunters find seal breathing holes in the ice, and protects the Inuit from muskoxen and polar bears. Its long outer coat, thick undercoat, and fur-covered feet allow this dog to survive in the hostile Arctic environment.

Ontario

Animal life thrives in Ontario, but the province has no official animal symbol. Ontario's forests are home to black bears, foxes, wildcats, and wolves. Caribou, deer, and moose are commonly seen in northern Ontario. White-tailed deer are common in the south, and polar bears roam along the shores of Hudson Bay in the North. Skunks, porcupines, rabbits, muskrats, beavers, and foxes can be found in all regions of the province.

Canada lynx live in the boreal forests of Ontario. The Canada lynx has long hair around its face, black-tipped ears, long hind legs, and a short tail. Its broad feet act like snowshoes by keeping the lynx from sinking into deep snow.

Prince Edward Island

Although Prince Edward Island has many types of animals, the province does not have an official animal symbol. Bears, bobcats, caribou, cougars, and moose once lived on Prince Edward Island. The black bear, which disappeared from the island in the 1920s, was the last large mammal in the province. Today, the most common mammals in Prince Edward Island are the raccoon, red squirrel, chipmunk, snowshoe hare, muskrat, red fox, and beaver.

Animals fill the waters surrounding Prince Edward Island. Atlantic white-sided dolphins and harbour porpoises frolic in the Northumberland Strait, just off High Bank and White Sands. Seals are another common sight. Harbour seals and grey seals are often seen near Panmure Island in the winter. Baby seals drift on floating sheets of ice each spring.

Quebec

Quebec is home to many animals, but has no official animal symbol. From polar bears to beavers, Quebec is home to a wide variety of animal life.

Large animals such as caribou, deer, black bears, and moose all live in Quebec's forests. Smaller animals in the province include skunks, raccoons, foxes, and squirrels. Beluga and blue whales thrill whale-watchers along the Gulf of Saint Lawrence. Harp seals can be found in the St. Lawrence Seaway. Grey seals, harbour porpoises, harbour seals, and minke whales also live in or visit the seaway.

Saskatchewan

The white-tailed deer became Saskatchewan's official animal in 2001. This deer lives in wooded areas throughout Saskatchewan. Though certain parts of its body remain white all year-round, it is reddish-brown in the summer and greyish-brown in the winter.

The white-tailed deer is a great jumper and a fast runner. It can run as fast as 50 to 60 kilometres per hour. The white-tailed deer is mostly active at night. Its diet mainly consists of green plants, nuts, and wood vegetation.

Yukon

The Yukon is home to a tremendous variety of animals, but the territory does not have an official animal. Beavers, martens, minks, and Arctic and red foxes can all be found in the territory. Wolves, hares, otters, lynxes, wolverines, coyotes, moose, muskoxen, bison, mountain goats, and elk also live in the Yukon. Seals, walruses, and whales swim off the Yukon's Arctic coast.

The porcupine caribou herd is one of the only herds of migrating barren-ground caribou left in the world. Each year, it travels 750 kilometres from the Arctic coast to the Yukon's southern mountain ranges. Woodland caribou also live in the territory. Wolves often follow the caribou herds.

One of North America's largest populations of Dall's sheep, or thinhorn sheep, makes its home in the Yukon's mountains. These sheep have a coat that provides warmth in the Yukon's climate. In the winter, their coats will often grow to more than 5 centimetres long.

Guide to Canada's Animals

THE NATIONAL ANIMAL
Beaver

ALBERTA
Rocky Mountain bighorn sheep

BRITISH COLUMBIA
Spirit bear

MANITOBA
Bison

NEW BRUNSWICK

NEWFOUNDLAND AND LABRADOR
Caribou

NORTHWEST TERRITORIES

NOVA SCOTIA
Duck tolling retriever

NUNAVUT
Canadian Inuit dog

ONTARIO

PRINCE EDWARD ISLAND

QUEBEC

SASKATCHEWAN
White-tailed deer

YUKON

Canada's National Animal Symbol

National emblems are symbols that are used for the entire country. The Canadian flag is one such symbol. Another is the common loon, which is the national bird. The national tree is the maple. Canada's national animal is the beaver.

The beaver is the largest rodent in North America. Its life span in nature is about 20 years.

Before the start of the fur trade, there were about six million beavers in Canada. Due to the fur trade, the beaver almost became **extinct** by the mid-19th century.

Today, due to conservation efforts, the beaver is alive and well all over the country.

National Animal History

In the late 1600s and early 1700s, the fashion of the day demanded fur hats made from beaver pelts. The trade of beaver pelts proved so profitable that the Hudson's Bay Company honoured the beaver by putting it on the shield of its coat of arms in 1678. On March 24, 1975, the beaver became a Canadian symbol.

Parts of the Beaver

Canada's national animal, the beaver, is among the most symbolically important symbols in the country.

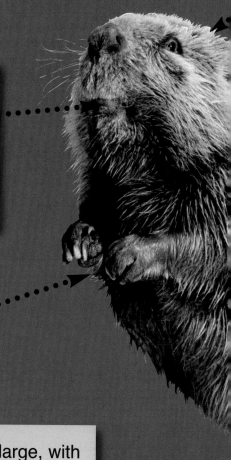

TEETH The beaver's teeth are long, sharp, strong incisors, which grow continuously. These teeth are hardened with a dark orange enamel. This is a glossy substance that covers teeth.

FOREPAWS The beaver's forepaws are small and delicate. Its toes end in long, sharp claws that are suitable for digging. Their paws are almost like hands. The beaver uses them to hold and carry sticks, stones, and mud.

HIND FEET The beaver's hind feet are very large, with five, long, blunt-clawed toes which are fully webbed for swimming. The beaver uses only its hind feet to move through water. Sometimes, it uses its tail to help propel itself. The second toe on each hind foot is double-clawed and acts like tiny pliers. These claws are used to comb the fur.

EYES The beaver's small, beady eyes can see as well in the water as they can on land. This is because of a special transparent, or clear, membrane that can be drawn over the eye for protection while diving.

FUR The dark brown fur, or pelt, of a beaver is very thick. It consists of a mat of fine underfur and an outer layer of heavy guard hairs. Through constant **preening** and oiling, this thick pelt is kept waterproof.

TAIL The beaver's tail has important uses both in the water and on land. Flexible and muscular, the tail of a large beaver may be 30 centimetres long, up to 18 centimetres wide, and 4 centimetres thick. The tail is covered with leathery scales and sparse, coarse hairs. On land, the tail acts as a **prop** when the beaver is sitting or standing upright.

Test Your Knowledge

4 When did the spirit bear become an official animal symbol in British Columbia?

1 What is Canada's national animal symbol?

2 What is Saskatchewan's faunal symbol?

5 Where can one of North America's largest populations of Dall's sheep be found?

3 In which province is the Mountain bighorn sheep an animal symbol?

6 What is Manitoba's animal symbol?

7 What colour are a beaver's teeth?

8 Which provinces and territories do not have official animal symbols?

9 When was the duck tolling retriever first bred in Nova Scotia?

13 Which animal symbol changes its colour in the winter?

14 Which province has two animal symbols?

10 What is special about the Canada lynx's feet?

15 What animal is on the Northwest Territories' license plate?

11 Which animal symbol appears on the Canadian five-cent coin?

12 What is another name for the Canadian Inuit dog?

Answers:
1. the beaver
2. the white-tailed deer
3. Alberta
4. April 2006
5. Yukon
6. the bison
7. Orange
8. New Brunswick, Northwest Territories, Ontario, Prince Edward Island, Quebec, Yukon
9. Early 1800s
10. They act like snowshoes.
11. The beaver
12. Qimmiq
13. The white-tailed deer
14. Newfoundland and Labrador
15. The polar bear

Create Your Own Animal Symbol

Create an animal symbol to represent you. Begin by thinking about what type of animal you want. Use this book to help you. Do you prefer animals that live on the ground, in water, or in trees?

Think about how you want your animal to look. Will it be a large or small animal? Will it eat meat or plants? What colour will it be? Look at the pictures in this book for help. You also can view some animal images online at **http://proudcanadian kids.ca/animals.htm**.

Draw your animal on a piece of paper. Use the diagram on pages 26 and 27 to help you design the parts of your animal. Colour your drawing with felt markers. When you are finished, label the parts of your animal.

Write a description of your animal. What kind of animal is it? Where does it live? What does it symbolize about you?

Further Research

Many books and websites provide information on animals in Canada. To learn more about these animals, borrow books from the library, or surf the Internet.

Books

Most libraries have computers that connect to a database for researching information. If you input a key word, you will be provided with a list of books in the library that contain information on that topic. Nonfiction books are arranged numerically, using their call number. Fiction books are organized alphabetically by the author's last name.

Websites

Find fun facts about each of Canada's provinces and territories at **www.pco-bcp.gc.ca/aia/index.asp?lang=eng&page= provterr&sub=map-carte&doc=map-carte-eng.htm**.

Learn about Canada's other symbols at **www.patrimoinecanadien.gc.ca/pgm/ceem-cced/symbl/ index-eng.cfm**.

To have some fun with the animals, visit **www.virtualmuseum.ca/Exhibitions/Emblemes/3000_e.php**.

Glossary ——— Index

albino: a person or animal lacking normal colouration

boreal: northern regions with very cold temperatures

breed: a group of organisms within a species

carrion: dead and rotting flesh

extinct: no longer existing any place on Earth

faunal: relating to all the animal life of a given place or time

First Nations: Canada's first inhabitants, or Aboriginal Peoples, with the exception of Inuit and Métis

genetic: a trait of an animal that is passed to younger generations

indigenous: from a certain place naturally

migratory: to move from one place to another

preening: smoothing or cleaning with the beak, bill, or tongue

prop: support placed beneath something to keep it from falling

robust: very strong

waterproof: not allowing water to pass through